W9-AHI-579

THE ART OF
SLUSH™

Creative & delicious recipes for slushies, milkshakes, smoothies, & more!

Jennifer Farley

Copyright © 2013 by Zoku, LLC
Photography copyright © 2013
by Zoku, LLC

Library of Congress Cataloging–in–Publication data is available.

Published by Zoku, LLC
720 Monroe Street, Suite C308
Hoboken, NJ 07030
www.zokuhome.com

ISBN: 978-0-988-31581-5

First Printing 2013

10 9 8 7 6 5 4 3 2 1

Printed in China

ART DIRECTOR
Ken Zorovich

BOOK DESIGNER
Theresa Lennahan

ADDITIONAL DESIGN AND PRODUCTION
James Farsetta

PHOTOGRAPHER
Melissa Goodwin

PHOTO RETOUCHING
Melissa Goodwin

FOOD STYLISTS
Yos Kumthampinij
Will Nickley
Mark Hearn

PROP STYLISTS
Yos Kumthampinij
Will Nickley

ADDITIONAL WRITING AND EDITING
Jackie Zorovich
Ken Zorovich

RECIPE TESTING AND CONSULTING
Trish Lobenfeld

We dedicate this book to all mothers for inspiring us and teaching us that, with hard work and perseverance, we can achieve our dreams.

TABLE OF contents

intro

the history of slush
8-9

introduction
10

ingredients and tips
11-13

slushies

kiwi pineappple
16-17

açai dream
18

fall's bounty
19

blood orange mojito
20-21

spicy bloody mary
22

carrot apple ginger
23

grapefruit bellini
24-25

pretty in pink beet juice
26-27

mandarin orange
28

orange energy
29

green refresher detox
30-31

the history of slush

THE BEGINNING OF TIME...

Researchers have found that the T. Rex could consume **FIVE HUNDRED** slushies a day. Thats a lot of slush!

1740

George Washington chopped down his father's cherry tree in his youth. When questioned, he said, "I cannot tell a lie, I chopped down the tree to make my favorite cherry slushy."

In the continental United States there are more than 1000 different varieties of cherry trees.

1922

World's first milkshake! In 1922, Walgreens' employee Ivar "Pop" Coulson added two scoops of vanilla ice cream to the standard malted milk recipe, and the milkshake as we know it was born!

By the 1950s, milkshakes were being sold at lunch counters, diners, burger joints, and drugstore soda fountains.

1950

Mom, where do slushies come from? Dairy Queen owner, Omar Knedlik, invented the slushy in the 1950s when his soda fountain broke down, forcing him to put his sodas in the freezer.

So many people loved these frozen sodas or "slushies" that Omar was inspired to invent a machine to make them.

Early prototypes for Omar's slushy machine used an automobile air conditioning unit to freeze the slushies.

WOW, WHO KNEW?

1969

One giant leap for slush kind!
On July 20, 1969 the first man and first slushy landed on the moon.

BUZZ ALDRIN & NEIL ARMSTRONG LOVED EATING TANG SLUSHIES IN SPACE

Slushy aliases: Slushies are also known as granitas, Slurpees, Slush Puppies, Icees, and Brain Freezes!

HELP

Placing your tongue on the roof of your mouth to warm the palate is one of the quickest ways to relieve

BRAIN FREEZE

1982

Hector Vargas, a science teacher at Ridgemont High School in California, invents the

CHILL PILL

after discovering the relaxing effect of slushies on his rowdy students. Gnarly dude!

What is a slushy?
Slushies are partially frozen water mixed with flavoring and sugar, without dairy products or eggs. Add egg and/or dairy and you've got ice cream, milkshakes, and smoothies!

Smoothies are often fruit-based, and come in every color of the rainbow. Don't discriminate—love smoothies of all colors and flavors!

TODAY

THE SLUSHY REVOLUTION BEGINS

ZOKU designed the Slush & Shake Maker, creating a quick and convenient way to enjoy a delicious slushy, milkshake, or smoothie in a matter of minutes.

WOW!

introduction

After forever changing the way people make ice pops with the Zoku Quick Pop Maker, the team at Zoku was inspired to start a Slushy Revolution. In our desire to live healthier and eat mindfully, we noticed that slushies (and slushy makers) had been left behind in the shuffle—sure they came in various colors and flavors, but they have certainly never been categorized as gourmet or healthy. That's why we're so excited to share these delicious, wholesome recipes for the Zoku Slush and Shake Maker with you.

The Art of Slush elevates frozen drinks to the next level with unique and appealing flavor combinations. Whether you're looking for a healthy, nutrient-packed slushy or you're in the mood to indulge with a decadent milkshake, we've got you covered. Enjoy a smoothie for breakfast, a slushy with lunch, and a shake for dessert! For a fun evening, you can impress your friends with one of our frozen cocktail recipes.

Of course you can make a great slushy just by pouring your favorite juice into the Slush and Shake Maker, but why stop there when there are so many fun and creative recipes to try? In this book, you'll find not only refreshing slushy recipes, but also mouth-watering recipes for smoothies, milkshakes, and even French fries—oh my!

We love to use fresh, wholesome ingredients to make slushies and smoothies that taste great, and are great for you (and we equally enjoy splurging with a milkshake and fries). Our favorite part of this Slushy Revolution is watching the smiles on peoples' faces as they see their drink freeze in just minutes inside the Zoku Slush and Shake Maker. Kids are especially delighted by the magical transformation—it's a fantastic way to spend quality time with children in the kitchen.

We had a lot of fun producing this book with Jennifer and we hope you enjoy these recipes as much as we do. Follow the recipes exactly, or if you're more adventurous, we encourage you to experiment and be creative!

ingredients

SWEETENERS

A wide assortment of sweeteners works great with the Slush and Shake Maker. We prefer using liquid sweeteners because granulated sugar does not dissolve well in cold or frozen beverages. Sugar and other powdered sweeteners may still be used, but keep in mind that they might not always disperse evenly. Superfine sugar is an instant-dissolving sugar, perfect for cold beverages, that is available in any grocery store. Light agave nectar is one of our favorite options for sweetening recipes because it is pale in color and neutral in flavor. It is quite different from, and not necessarily interchangeable with, amber agave nectar, which has a color similar to maple syrup and a very distinct flavor. Other liquid sweeteners such as honey, maple syrup, and simple syrup (a mixture of equal parts sugar and water that has been simmered until the sugar dissolves) work great in slush and shake recipes too. Sweetened condensed milk is another delicious option that adds both sweetness and dairy to a recipe. Recipes with a lot of sweetener will generally take longer to freeze since sugar lowers the freezing point.

DAIRY

Many of the recipes in this book call for some kind of dairy or dairy-alternative beverage. Each recipe highlights the ingredient that we think will work best in that particular drink, but feel free to make substitutions. Heavy cream, half and half, whole milk, 2%, 1%, and fat-free milk all can be used interchangeably; the flavor and consistency will vary accordingly. Half and half and whole milk are typically the best options because they are creamy without being overly heavy. Whole fat and Greek yogurts work best in smoothies due to their distinct tangy flavor. When yogurt and fruit are combined, they should be added to the Slush and Shake Maker immediately; the acid from the fruit eventually curdles the yogurt, which does not affect the flavor, just the appearance. Excellent dairy alternatives include coconut milk, soy milk, rice milk, and almond milk (almond milk is our favorite due to its neutral flavor).

FRUIT

We recommend using ripe, organic, seasonal produce whenever possible. If you're able to find fresh strawberries at the market in the middle of winter, you'll notice that they are never as sweet as those in season. In addition to being much sweeter, a ripe peach also has a much smoother texture than an under-ripe peach when pureed. Even bananas turn sweeter as they ripen. That's why we recommend sweetening beverages to taste before adding them to the Slush and Shake Maker. If a recipe calls for 1 teaspoon of light agave nectar, it might very well need 2 or 3 teaspoons if the fruit is out of season or under-ripe. Or you may not need to add any sweetener if the fruit is ripe. Fruit canned in its own juice, not in syrup, is another good option.

ALCOHOL

Several recipes in this book include an option to add alcohol for an adult version of the drink. Look for the martini icon throughout the book next to recipes that have an option for alcohol. Alcohol lowers the freezing point of liquid, so recipes with alcohol will take longer to freeze. For best results, we recommend adding the alcohol after the drink has begun to freeze. Adding the alcohol will cause the frozen mixture to melt, but if you continue stirring, the slush will refreeze after a few minutes.

GENERAL TIPS

For best results, freeze your Zoku Slush and Shake Maker overnight before using it for the first time. Read the product instructions carefully. Always make sure that your ingredients are cold before adding them to the Slush and Shake Maker. The colder the ingredients, the faster each recipe freezes. For the best consistency, stir frequently, and gently scrape the walls of the Slush and Shake Maker with the included spoon while waiting for the drink to freeze. Before adding frozen ingredients such as ice cream or frozen fruit to the blender, microwave them for 15 to 30 seconds to soften them up. When you puree ingredients on high speed, the liquid expands in volume due to the air bubbles that get trapped in the mixture (as with egg white meringues, for example). Before adding blended drinks to the Slush and Shake Maker, allow them to settle for a minute. Alternatively, you can continue adding the drink to the Slush and Shake Maker while enjoying your slushy. All specialty ingredients used in the recipes can be found at gourmet specialty shops or through online retailers.

LET'S GO!

slush

ies

kiwi pineapple
açai dream
fall's bounty
blood orange mojito
spicy bloody mary
carrot apple ginger
grapefruit bellini
pretty in pink beet juice
mandarin orange
orange energy
green refresher detox
concord grape
cherry
purple antioxidant berry
tropical paradise
sangria
strawberry lemonade
peppermint latte
horchata
chocolate amaretto
vietnamese iced coffee
lavender hot chocolate

KIWI
PINEAPPLE
SLUSH

KIWI PINEAPPLE **SLUSH**

There's really only one word for this kiwi pineapple slushy: refreshing. Any non-dairy milk can be used in this recipe but we caution against using dairy products such as yogurt or milk. Believe it or not, there's an enzyme in both kiwis and pineapples that reacts with dairy to create a bitter aftertaste. You will find no such bitterness in this dairy-free version.

Serves 2

INGREDIENTS:

1 heaping cup (6 ounces) chopped pineapple

1 cup almond milk or non-dairy substitute

2 kiwis, peeled

1/4 cup pineapple juice

1 tablespoon freshly squeezed lime juice

1 teaspoon light agave nectar

DIRECTIONS:

Purée the pineapple, milk, kiwis, pineapple juice, lime juice, and agave nectar in a blender. Pour into the Slush and Shake Maker; stir until thick.

"Açai fruit are small, flavorful berries that are packed with antioxidants."

AÇAI DREAM
SLUSH

Açai fruit are small, flavorful berries that are packed with antioxidants. 100% açai juice can be found in most supermarkets and it makes a wonderful base for smoothies and slushies. In this slushy we've paired it with orange and pomegranate juice for added brightness and a touch of acidity.

Serves 2

INGREDIENTS:

1 cup 100% açai juice

1/2 cup freshly squeezed orange juice (approximately 1 large or 2 small oranges)

1/2 cup pomegranate juice

DIRECTIONS:

Stir together the açai juice, orange juice, and pomegranate juice. Pour into the Slush and Shake Maker; stir until thick.

FALL'S BOUNTY
SLUSH

There's something about fall fruit that brings us so much joy. Pears and apples are in their prime during the crisp autumn months and this is the absolute best time to juice them. We recommend using Granny Smith apples in this recipe, but any tart apple will work well.

Serves 2

INGREDIENTS:

4 Bosc pears, quartered

4 Granny Smith apples, quartered

40 green seedless grapes (approximately 7 ounces)

DIRECTIONS:

Juice the fruit in batches; stir to combine. Pour into the Slush and Shake Maker; stir until thick.

"Pears and apples are in their prime during the crisp autumn months."

BLOOD ORANGE MOJITO
SPARKLING SLUSH

Blood oranges are a seasonal treat that infuse this slushy with a bold, ruby red color. They are slightly smaller than regular oranges and have a unique flavor profile with notes of tangy raspberry. If you are unable to find blood oranges, substitute regular varieties of oranges.

Serves 2

INGREDIENTS:

25 mint leaves, divided

1/2 cup sugar

1/2 cup water

1/2 cup blood orange juice (approximately 6 blood oranges; regular oranges may be substituted)

2 tablespoons fresh lime juice (1 to 2 limes)

1 cup sparkling water

optional: 2 fluid ounces rum, divided

DIRECTIONS:

To make a mint simple syrup, heat up the sugar, water, and 15 mint leaves in a small saucepan over medium heat. Allow the mixture to simmer for 3 minutes and remove from the heat. Without removing the mint, chill the simple syrup for at least an hour in the refrigerator. Strain and discard the mint. Stir the simple syrup together with the blood orange juice, lime juice, sparkling water, and remaining mint leaves. Pour into the Slush and Shake Makers. Stir until slushy and then add 1 fluid ounce rum, if using, into each Maker. The mixture will thin out; continue to stir until thick.

SPICY BLOODY MARY
SLUSH

Bloody Marys are the ultimate drink for lazy weekend brunches. We've spiced up the traditional version with Old Bay and cayenne pepper for a slushy that will be sure to wake you up!

Serves 2

INGREDIENTS:

1 1/2 cups tomato juice

1/4 cup lemon juice (approximately 2 lemons)

2 tablespoons olive juice, from a jar of green olives

2 teaspoons Worcestershire sauce

1/2 teaspoon Old Bay seasoning

6 to 8 shakes Tabasco sauce

1/4 teaspoon cayenne pepper, or to taste

optional: 3 fluid ounces vodka, divided

optional: celery for garnish

DIRECTIONS:

Whisk the tomato juice, lemon juice, olive juice, Worcestershire sauce, Old Bay seasoning, Tabasco, and cayenne in a medium bowl. Pour the mixture into the Slush and Shake Makers; stir until thick. Add 1 1/2 ounces vodka, if using, to each Slush and Shake Maker and stir to combine. The mixture will thin out; continue to stir until thick. Garnish with celery, if using.

CARROT APPLE GINGER
SLUSH

This delightfully healthy juicer recipe is a great way to get vitamins and minerals into your diet. Ginger has many known health benefits, including preventing colds, reducing inflammation, and soothing upset stomachs. Plus it adds an invigorating spiciness to this slushy.

Serves 2

INGREDIENTS:

12 ounces carrots (approximately
  5 to 6 medium carrots), chopped
4 Granny Smith apples, quartered
1/2 inch cube of ginger

DIRECTIONS:

Juice the produce in batches; stir to combine.
Pour into the Slush and Shake Maker; stir until thick.

GRAPEFRUIT BELLINI
COCKTAIL

When we think of sparkling wine, we think of parties, elegance, and fun. This grapefruit Bellini cocktail is ideal for toasting or celebrating any day of the year. Try stirring a few mint leaves into the slushy for an added twist. For best results, use freshly squeezed grapefruit juice instead of the store-bought variety.

Serves 2

INGREDIENTS:

1 1/4 cups freshly squeezed pink grapefruit juice (approximately 3 grapefruits), divided

3/4 cup Prosecco, divided

optional: fresh mint leaves for garnish

DIRECTIONS:

Divide the grapefruit juice evenly between the two Slush and Shake Makers; stir until thick. Add 6 tablespoons Prosecco to each Slush and Shake Maker. Stir to combine. The mixture will thin out; continue to stir until thick. Garnish with mint, if using.

PRETTY IN PINK BEET JUICE **SLUSH**

This gorgeous, bright pink slushy is sweet yet refreshingly tart. As a bonus, the detoxifying beet juice is full of vitamins and minerals. If you're looking for an energy boost, this slushy is for you.

"If you're looking for an energy boost, this slushy is for you."

Serves 2

INGREDIENTS:

5 cups (20 ounces) hulled strawberries

2 oranges, peeled and quartered

2 sweet apples, such as Gala or Fuji, quartered

1 large or 2 small beets (~5 ounces with stems and root end removed), scrubbed clean and cut into thin slices

1 small lemon, peeled

DIRECTIONS:

Juice the strawberries, oranges, apples, beets, and lemon; stir to combine. Pour into the Slush and Shake Maker; stir until thick.

MANDARIN ORANGE
SLUSH

This exotic twist on an orange slushy is sure to be a crowd pleaser. The mandarin oranges add a bright and tangy flavor. If you are ever lucky enough to find fresh mandarin oranges, be sure to give them a try in this recipe.

Serves 2

INGREDIENTS:

1 1/2 cups freshly squeezed orange juice (approximately 6 medium oranges)

1 can (10.5 ounces) mandarin oranges in juice, drained

optional: 1/4 teaspoon orange blossom water

DIRECTIONS:

Puree all of the ingredients in a blender. Pour into Slush and Shake Maker; stir until thick.

ORANGE ENERGY
BLAST

With the color of a beautiful sunrise and a blast of vitamins, this slushy is a healthy way to jump-start your morning. Plus, it's absolutely delicious. Who needs caffeine when this little potion will wake you right up? Also try this recipe for a late afternoon pick-me-up!

Serves 2

INGREDIENTS:
- 1 large or 2 small grapefruit (approximately 1 pound), peeled and quartered
- 2 large oranges (approximately 1 pound), peeled and quartered
- 2 sweet apples* (approximately 11 ounces), quartered
- 1/2 pound carrots, washed and chopped
- 3/4 cup hulled strawberries

DIRECTIONS:
Juice the produce in batches; stir to combine. Pour into Slush and Shake Maker; stir until thick.

* The perfect sweet apple: We recommend Gala or Fuji apples for this recipe.

GREEN REFRES
DETOX SLUSH

Your body will thank you for making this detoxifying slushy to boost its natural cleansing process. There are many foods that aid in detoxification, and we've created a slushy that highlights a few of these ingredients: cucumber, apples, kale, and lime.

GREEN REFRESHER DETOX **SLUSH**

Serves 2

INGREDIENTS:

2 large cucumbers

2 Granny Smith apples, quartered

2 cups (approximately 3 ounces) tightly packed kale, rinsed and stems removed

1 lime, peeled

DIRECTIONS:

Juice the cucumbers, apples, kale, and lime; stir to combine. Pour into the Slush and Shake Maker; stir until thick.

CONCORD GRAPE
SPARKLING SLUSH

Channel your inner child and bring back fond memories of drinking grape soda during care-free, barefoot summers. Hold onto that feeling, but this time around, you can skip the artificial ingredients for a guilt-free slushy packed with antioxidants and vitamin C.

Serves 2

INGREDIENTS:
1 1/4 cups 100% concord grape juice
3/4 cup club soda
1 tablespoon freshly squeezed lemon juice
pinch of salt

DIRECTIONS:
Stir together the grape juice, club soda, lemon juice, and salt. Pour into the Slush and Shake Maker; stir until thick.

"Bring back fond memories of care-free, barefoot summers."

CHERRY SPARKLING **SLUSH**

It'll take you only a few seconds to whip up this thirst-quenching sparkling slushy using bottled cherry juice. If you're feeling inspired, you can try juicing pitted cherries. For a Roy Rodgers twist, try replacing the club soda with regular cola.

Serves 2

INGREDIENTS:

1 cup 100% cherry juice

1 cup club soda

1 tablespoon lime juice

DIRECTIONS:

Stir together the cherry juice, club soda, and lime juice. Pour into the Slush and Shake Maker; stir until thick.

PURPLE ANTIOXIDANT
BERRY BLAST

It's quite possible that berries are one of the tastiest health foods on the market. They're low in calories and full of the good stuff—vitamin C, calcium, potassium and a host of other vitamins and minerals. Double the servings by adding sparkling water for a homemade berry soda.

Serves 2

INGREDIENTS:

1 pint (8 ounces) blackberries

1 pint (8 ounces) blueberries

2 cups (8 ounces) hulled strawberries

1 sweet apple, such as Gala or Fuji, quartered

DIRECTIONS:

Juice the berries and apple; stir to combine. Pour into the Slush and Shake Maker; stir until thick.

TROPICAL PARADISE
SLUSH

After a day of fun in the Caribbean sun (or just close your eyes, relax, and imagine), you can chill out with this tropical treat. Peel the fruit as noted before juicing to ensure a smooth finish.

Serves 2

INGREDIENTS:

2 mangoes (approximately 1 1/2 pounds), peeled and pits removed

2 oranges (approximately 1 pound), peeled and quartered

2 kiwis (approximately 5 to 6 ounces), peeled

1 sweet apple, such as Gala or Fuji (6 to 7 ounces), quartered

DIRECTIONS:

Juice the fruit in batches; stir to combine. Pour into the Slush and Shake Maker; stir until thick.

SANGR

SANGRIA **SLUSH**

Serves 2

INGREDIENTS:

1 cup freshly squeezed orange juice (approximately 4 juice oranges or 2 navel oranges)

1/4 cup freshly squeezed lemon juice (approximately 1 large lemon)

2 tablespoons superfine sugar

7 fluid ounces fruity Spanish red wine, divided

DIRECTIONS:

Whisk together the orange juice, lemon juice, and sugar in a small bowl. Continue stirring until the sugar dissolves, about 2 minutes. Divide the juice evenly between the two Slush and Shake Makers; stir until thick. Add 3 1/2 ounces of wine to each Maker and stir to combine. The mixture will thin out; continue to stir until thick.

IA SLUSH

Sangria is one of our favorite summer drinks and this refreshing slush is perfect for outdoor parties! We recommend using an inexpensive fruity wine with good acidity. There's no need to spend a lot of money since the wine will be mixed with other ingredients, but don't choose something you wouldn't normally drink. Spanish reds work well.

STRAWBERRY LEMONADE **SLUSH**

Strawberries and lemonade—can you feel your cheeks start to pucker, or what? The whole family will love this summery slushy. There's just nothing better on a hot, sunny day.

Serves 2

INGREDIENTS:

2 cups (8 ounces) hulled and sliced strawberries

6 tablespoons freshly squeezed lemon juice, strained (approximately 2 large lemons)

1/3 cup superfine sugar* or 2 tablespoons light agave nectar

1/2 cup cold water

DIRECTIONS:

Purée the strawberries, lemon juice, sugar, and water in a blender. Pour into the Slush and Shake Maker; stir until thick.

> * Superfine sugar is an instant-dissolving sugar, perfect for cold beverages, that is available at any grocery store.

PEPPERMINT LATTE
SLUSH

Many of the recipes in this book take advantage of fresh mint, but there's just something about peppermint extract that's very reminiscent of the holiday season. Perhaps the abundance of candy canes? We thought that would be divine mixed with some espresso and milk to create a fun holiday treat. The extract can be quite strong, so use it sparingly. Also, be sure to stir frequently while the slushy freezes because the oil will try to separate from the espresso and milk. If using just two shots of espresso, the drinks will not reach the fill lines, so add some more milk if you'd like.

Serves 2

INGREDIENTS:

1 1/4 cups whole milk

1/4 cup superfine sugar

2 to 4 shots freshly brewed espresso

1/4 to 1/2 teaspoon peppermint extract, or to taste

garnish: crushed candy canes or peppermint candies

DIRECTIONS:

Whisk the milk, sugar, espresso, and peppermint until the sugar dissolves, about 2 minutes. Pour into the Slush and Shake Maker; stir until thick. Garnish with crushed candy.

HORCHATA **SLUSH**

Those who have never visited Mexico or the Southwestern U.S. might not be familiar with the popular Mexican rice drink known as horchata. Sweet, milky, and earthy, horchata is an unexpected treat that lends itself perfectly to a scrumptious slushy. You can find store-bought versions that will work in the Slush and Shake Maker, but homemade horchata is simple to prepare and has the best flavor.

"Sweet, milky, and earthy, horchata is an unexpected treat."

Serves 2

INGREDIENTS:

1/2 cup white long grain basmati rice

2 cups lukewarm water

1/2 cup full fat sweetened condensed milk

3/4 teaspoon cinnamon

1/2 teaspoon vanilla extract

DIRECTIONS:

In a blender, purée the rice and water for about a minute on high speed to break up the grains. Allow the mixture to steep for at least 2 to 3 hours. Strain the liquid into a large measuring cup or bowl through a cheesecloth or nut milk bag. Discard the rice. Whisk the sweetened condensed milk, cinnamon, and vanilla extract into the liquid. The cinnamon will float on top. Pour into the Slush and Shake Maker, using a spoon to disperse the cinnamon evenly; stir until thick.

CHOCOLATE AMARET

CHOCOLATE AMARETTO **SLUSH**

Serves 2

INGREDIENTS:

1 3/4 cups almond milk

2 tablespoons mild honey, such as Acacia

1 tablespoon unsweetened cocoa powder

1/2 teaspoon vanilla extract

1/4 cup Amaretto, divided

DIRECTIONS:

Heat the almond milk in a small saucepan over medium heat. Once hot, whisk in the cocoa powder and honey. Cool, then refrigerate until cold, about 1 hour. Stir in the vanilla. Pour into the Slush and Shake Makers; stir until thick. Add 2 tablespoons Amaretto to each Maker; stir to combine. The mixture will thin out; continue to stir until thick.

O SLUSH

Amaretto is a sweet, almond-flavored liqueur, which pairs beautifully with chocolate in this fun, light cocktail. We've used almond milk to play on the almond liqueur, but any milk or half and half also works well here for a richer version.

VIETNAMESE ICED COFFEE **SLUSH**

Vietnamese iced coffee, locally known as "ca phe sua da", is an incredibly creamy and delectable drink. Sweetened condensed milk replaces the usual cream and sugar, while strong French roast coffee balances the sweetness. Coffee with chicory is traditionally used in this icy drink, adding a smooth chocolate undertone; however, any strong dark roast works well. This recipe requires no special equipment but if you'd like to try making authentic Vietnamese iced coffee, special filters are available online and in Asian markets.

"Vietnamese iced coffee is an incredibly creamy & delectable drink."

Serves 2

INGREDIENTS:

2 cups filtered water

3/4 cup ground dark roast coffee

1/2 cup sweetened condensed milk

DIRECTIONS:

Bring the water to a boil in medium-sized saucepan. Add the coffee, stir to incorporate, and let steep 5 minutes. Strain the coffee through a cheesecloth-lined strainer into a clean container. Strain again if you see any coffee grounds in the coffee. Cool, then refrigerate until cold, about 1 hour. Whisk in the condensed milk. Pour into the Slush and Shake Maker; stir until thick.

LAVENDER HOT CHOCOLATE **SLUSH**

Lavender infuses this slushy with a calming floral flavor that will have you cozying up with this cool treat. A superb complement to chocolate, lavender is lovely in this soothing slushy. Dried lavender can be found online and at many spice shops.

Serves 2

INGREDIENTS:

1/4 cup granulated sugar

1/4 cup cold water

2 tablespoons dried lavender

2 cups whole milk

2 1/2 tablespoons unsweetened cocoa powder

DIRECTIONS:

To make a lavender simple syrup, place the sugar, water, and lavender in a medium-sized pot over medium heat and bring to a boil. Lower the heat and simmer 5 minutes; turn off the heat and let sit 15 minutes. Strain the syrup through a cheesecloth-lined strainer into a clean container. Cool, then chill in the refrigerator until cold, about 1 hour. Put the simple syrup and milk in a clean saucepan over medium heat. Once the milk is hot, whisk in the cocoa powder, stirring until dissolved. Cool the mixture, then refrigerate until cold, about 1 hour. Stir the mixture and pour it into the Slush and Shake Maker; stir until thick.

milk
sh

cookies & cream

chocolate peanut butter cup

strawberry milkshake

classic fries

malted vanilla bean

eggnog rum

chai soy latte

toasted coconut

bananas foster

pistachio cardamom

espresso vodka dark chocolate

floats

nakes

COOKIES & CREAM
MILKSHAKE

Cookies and cream is a classic combination. Is it even possible to improve on such perfection? We think so! Cookie butter, also known as "speculoos", is sold in supermarkets by numerous brands such as Biscoff and Trader Joe's. It's still new to many people, but has been gaining popularity because it's downright delicious. We could eat this stuff with a spoon! It has a silky smooth consistency similar to peanut butter, with a sweet taste reminiscent of graham crackers. Adding just a spoonful to vanilla ice cream creates an amazing base for a cookie-flavored milkshake. Stir in some chopped up Oreos and you have one mouth-watering milkshake.

Serves 2

INGREDIENTS:

1 cup vanilla ice cream

1/2 cup whole milk

optional: 2 tablespoons cookie butter, such as Biscoff

1/2 cup chopped Oreo cookies (approximately 5 cookies), divided

garnish: 2 Oreo cookies

DIRECTIONS:

Purée the ice cream, milk, and cookie butter, if using. Pour into the Slush and Shake Makers and add one-half of the chopped Oreos to each Maker; stir until thick. Garnish with an Oreo.

CHOCOLATE PEANUT BUTTER CUP
MILKSHAKE

What's not to love about chocolate and peanut butter? Peanut butter cups create a nice texture in this luscious milkshake. We recommend using two regular-sized cups. If you use mini or king-sized peanut butter cups, scale according to taste.

Serves 2

INGREDIENTS:
3/4 cup chocolate ice cream
1/4 cup heavy cream
2 tablespoons creamy peanut butter
1 teaspoon light agave nectar
2 (1.1 ounce) regular-sized peanut butter cups, chopped and divided

DIRECTIONS:
Purée the ice cream, peanut butter, and agave nectar in a blender. Pour into the Slush and Shake Makers and add one chopped peanut butter cup to each Maker; stir until thickened.

STRAW
BERRY

STRAWBERRY
MILKSHAKE
with Grand Marnier

Grand Marnier is an orange-flavored brandy liqueur that is commonly added to desserts, sauces, and an assortment of mixed drinks. It pairs well with vanilla and strawberries, which is why we thought it would be an excellent addition to this milkshake. If you'd prefer to keep this drink alcohol-free, simply add an additional 1 1/2 tablespoons of freshly squeezed orange juice in place of the liqueur.

Serves 2

INGREDIENTS:

1 container (16 ounces) strawberries, hulled and sliced

1 cup vanilla ice cream

1/4 cup freshly squeezed orange juice

optional: 2 tablespoons Grand Marnier, divided

DIRECTIONS:

Purée the strawberries, ice cream, and orange juice in a blender. Pour into the Slush and Shake Makers; stir until thick. Add 1 tablespoon Grand Marnier, if using, to each Slush and Shake Maker. Stir to combine; the mixture will thin out, continue to stir until thick.

classic fries

CLASSIC **FRIES**

Would you like fries with that shake? These French fries are spectacular dunked in any of our milkshakes for a playful mix of sweet and savory. We recommend using a high-quality mandoline to create fast-food-sized fries, optimal for dipping into your shake. Also, make sure to always keep the peeled, sliced potatoes in cold water before using to prevent oxidation.

NOTES

Temperature control is important to well-prepared fries. Cook in batches; overcrowding the pot decreases the temperature dramatically. If the oil is too hot, it will overcook the outside of the fries and undercook the inside. If the temperature is too low, the fries will soak up the oil and become greasy and soggy.

Serves 2

INGREDIENTS:

3 large russet potatoes, peeled

2 quarts high heat neutral oil, such as canola, grape seed, or sunflower oil

salt to taste

DIRECTIONS:

Prepare a large bowl of ice water and set aside. Use a mandoline with the appropriate attachment to cut potatoes into thin French fries. Place the cut potatoes into the ice water. Cover and refrigerate for at least 45 minutes or overnight. Heat the oil in a 4-quart Dutch oven or heavy bottomed saucepan. Clip a frying thermometer to the pot and bring to 325 degrees F. Drain the potatoes and lay on a dish towel-lined cookie tray. Dry thoroughly; any residual water will cause the hot oil to bubble over. Line another tray with paper towels. Add 1/3 of the fries to the hot oil (325 degrees F) and blanch by cooking for 6 minutes. Adjust the flame as needed to maintain a constant temperature. Remove the fries with a slotted spoon to the paper towel-lined tray. Repeat until all of the fries are blanched. Remove the dish towel and line the tray with paper towels. Increase the temperature of the oil to 350 degrees F. Add one-half of the blanched fries to the hot oil and cook until golden brown. Remove the fries with a slotted spoon to the freshly lined tray and season with salt to taste; keep warm. Cook the remaining potatoes, remove, and season.

MALTED VANILLA BEAN **MILKSHAKE**

MALTED VANILLA BEAN **MILKSHAKE**

There's something very indulgent about using real vanilla beans in a vanilla milkshake. Their rich flavor and unique speckled appearance elevate this vanilla milkshake to gourmet status. Vanilla bean paste, which can be found online and at specialty stores, also works well to provide an intense fragrant flavor that's superior to regular extract. If you're in a pinch, you can substitute 2 teaspoons vanilla extract for the beans or paste.

Serves 2

INGREDIENTS:

1 cup vanilla ice cream

1 cup half and half

2 tablespoons malted milk powder

2 vanilla beans, or 2 tablespoons
vanilla bean paste

DIRECTIONS:

To separate the seeds from the vanilla bean pods, place each bean on a cutting board. Use a small paring knife to split the bean pods in half lengthwise. Use the knife to scrape out the seeds by pressing it along the split bean pod on an angle. In a blender, combine the ice cream, malt powder, half and half, and all of the vanilla bean seeds. Pour into the Slush and Shake Maker; stir until thick.

EGGNOG RUM
MILKSHAKE

There are so many reasons to get excited about the holiday season each year, and for us it's all about the food! Eggnog is so incredibly decadent that its limited availability is (almost) understandable. The creamy custard base of eggnog lends itself superbly to milkshakes. For a lighter version that is more of a slushy consistency, try using soy nog instead.

Serves 2

INGREDIENTS:

1 3/4 cups eggnog or soy nog
1 teaspoon cinnamon
optional: 2 fluid ounces spiced rum, such as Captain Morgan, divided
garnish: dash of nutmeg

DIRECTIONS:

Add the cinnamon to the measuring cup with the eggnog and whisk until blended. Pour into the Slush and Shake Makers; stir until thick. Add 1 tablespoon of rum, if using, to each Slush and Shake Maker. Stir to combine. The mixture will thin out; continue to stir until thick. Garnish with a dash of nutmeg.

CHAI SOY LATTE

CHAI SOY LATTE
MILKSHAKE

Chai is a delicious tea drink typically made by combining black tea with an assortment of aromatic spices. Coffee houses will often serve chai lattes for those seeking an alternative to espresso drinks. For those looking to enjoy chai at home, many grocery stores sell boxes with individual chai bags as well as loose versions of the tea. Powdered mixes that can be added to hot milk are also available. For this milkshake we've infused chai spices twice: first while creating a chai simple syrup, and again when blending the milkshake. The result is an exotic milkshake full of wonderful spices.

Serves 2

INGREDIENTS:

6 tablespoons granulated sugar

1/2 cup cold water

1 tablespoon loose black tea (2 to 3 tea bags)

1 cinnamon stick

2 cardamom pods, smashed

1 whole clove

1 cup soy milk

1 cup vanilla soy ice cream

1/4 teaspoon ground cardamom

1/4 teaspoon ground cinnamon

pinch of ground cloves

garnish: 2 cinnamon sticks

DIRECTIONS:

To make a chai simple syrup, place the sugar, water, tea, cinnamon stick, cardamom pods, and whole clove in a medium-sized pot over medium heat and bring to a boil. Lower the heat and simmer 3 minutes. Strain the syrup through a cheesecloth-lined strainer into a clean container. Cool, then chill in the refrigerator until cold, about 1 hour. Purée the syrup, milk, ice cream, and ground spices in a blender. Pour into the Slush and Shake Maker; stir until thick. Garnish with a cinnamon stick.

TOASTED COCONUT
MILKSHAKE

There are an abundance of non-dairy ice creams on the market these days and they open up so many dessert possibilities. We were inspired after tasting a rich vanilla coconut milk ice cream. The flavor was so wonderfully intense that we decided to use it as the base for a dairy-free coconut milkshake. Coconut milk, toasted sweetened coconut flakes, and coconut rum are combined with coconut ice cream to create the ultimate coconut taste explosion! For a vegan milkshake, try using light agave nectar instead of honey.

Serves 2

INGREDIENTS:
1/3 cup sweetened coconut flakes
1 1/3 cups dairy-free vanilla coconut ice cream
1/2 cup coconut milk
2 tablespoons mild honey, such as Acacia
1/2 teaspoon cinnamon
optional: 2 fluid ounces coconut rum,
  such as Malibu, divided

DIRECTIONS:
Preheat the oven to 350 degrees F. Spread the coconut flakes evenly across a baking sheet and toast in preheated oven until golden brown (5 to 10 minutes). Watch carefully; when the coconut starts to brown, it goes quickly. Purée the coconut flakes, ice cream, coconut milk, honey, and cinnamon in a blender. Pour into the Slush and Shake Makers; stir until thick. Add 1 tablespoon rum, if using, to each Slush and Shake Maker. Stir to combine. The mixture will thin out; continue to stir until thick.

BANANAS FOSTER
MILKSHAKE

Bananas Foster is a dessert with bananas and vanilla ice cream, topped with a sauce made with butter, brown sugar, cinnamon, and rum. Traditionally, the rum is ignited in a flambé pan, creating dramatic flames. If you think that sounds delicious, just wait until you try this milkshake—it's served cold, but the taste is on fire!

Serves 2

INGREDIENTS:
2 tablespoons unsalted butter
1/4 cup brown sugar
1/4 teaspoon cinnamon
1/4 teaspoon allspice
7 ounces sliced banana (1 large
   or 2 small bananas)
optional: 2 tablespoons rum
2/3 cup heavy cream
2/3 cup vanilla ice cream
1/4 cup chopped walnuts

DIRECTIONS:
Put the butter in a large sauté pan over medium heat. As it starts to melt, stir in the brown sugar, cinnamon, and allspice. Add the bananas and stir to coat with the sugar and butter. Add the rum, if using, and stir to combine. Pour in the cream and stir. Remove from heat as soon as the mixture is creamy and blended. Purée the warm banana mixture and the ice cream in a blender. Add the walnut and pulse to just combine, leaving pieces for texture. Pour into the Slush and Shake Maker; stir until thick.

PISTACHIO CARDAMOM **MILKSHAKE**

Cardamom and pistachios are made for each other, so we've played cupid, bringing them together in this distinctive milkshake. Cardamom is one of those magical spices that can be used in a wide variety of both sweet and savory dishes. It can be found in grocery stores and specialty spice shops in three forms: as pods, seeds, and finely ground powder. If you have a spice grinder, freshly ground cardamom seeds have the best flavor (pre-ground works great too).

Serves 2

INGREDIENTS:

3 tablespoons shelled raw pistachios, divided

1 1/2 cups pistachio ice cream

1/2 cup half and half

1 teaspoon light agave nectar

1/2 teaspoon ground cardamom

DIRECTIONS:

Preheat the oven to 350 degrees F. Toast the pistachios until they smell fragrant and are golden in color, 5 to 7 minutes. Coarsely chop the nuts and set aside. In a blender, purée the ice cream, half and half, agave, and cardamom. Pour into the Slush and Shake Makers and add 1 1/2 tablespoons pistachios to each Maker; stir until thick.

PISTACHIO
CARDAMOM
MILKSHAKE

ESPRESSO VODKA DARK CHOCOLATE **MILKSHAKE**

Espresso-infused vodka is sold on the market by several brands. It's always surprisingly smooth compared to regular vodka. Since coffee and chocolate are such a natural pairing, we've combined double espresso vodka with dark chocolate ice cream for an intense, adult twist on the classic chocolate milkshake. Espresso powder is an ingredient that bakers often add to chocolate dishes and we've used it here to further enhance the flavor. Espresso powder can be found online and in specialty shops. If you cannot locate it or wish to omit it from the recipe, unsweetened cocoa powder can also be added in its place.

Serves 2

INGREDIENTS:

1 cup dark chocolate ice cream

1/2 cup regular sweetened condensed milk

1/2 cup heavy cream

1/4 teaspoon vanilla extract

optional: 1 teaspoon espresso powder or unsweetened cocoa powder

2 fluid ounces espresso vodka, such as Van Gogh, divided

DIRECTIONS:

Purée the ice cream, condensed milk, cream, vanilla extract, and espresso powder, if using. Pour into the Slush and Shake Makers; stir until thick. Add 1 ounce espresso vodka to each Slush and Shake Maker. Stir to combine. The mixture will thin out; continue to stir until thick.

FLOAT

Serves 2

INGREDIENTS:
1 1/3 cups root beer
1 cup vanilla ice cream

DIRECTIONS:
Purée the root beer and vanilla ice cream in a blender. Pour into the Slush and Shake Maker; stir until thick.

Try swapping out the root beer for...

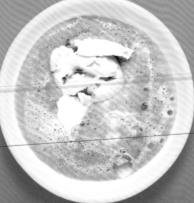

GRAPE SODA

Ice cream can be added after the soda is poured

ORANGE SODA

Garnish with an orange slice and whipped cream

ROOT BEER FLOAT
MILKSHAKE

We get nostalgic over root beer floats and we love using the Slush and Shake Maker for a modern twist. For this recipe we've combined the ice cream and root beer together in a blender to create a more classic milkshake. To make a more traditional root beer float, add 1 scoop (1/2 cup) of vanilla ice cream to each Slush and Shake Maker, then pour the root beer to the fill line and stir until thick. Periodically, you can add more soda while enjoying the milkshake. Be sure to experiment with the ingredients! This recipe works great with cream sodas and colas. For an adult version, try stout beer and chocolate ice cream.

STOUT BEER
Swap out the vanilla ice cream for chocolate

COLA
Top with whipped cream and add a cherry

CHERRY COLA
Try pouring soda on top of the ice cream

smoo

othies

peaches & cream
cherry pomegranate
banana caramel
key lime avocado
banana nutella
roasted strawberry balsamic
mango lassi
piña colada

PEACHES & CREAM
SMOOTHIE

Peaches and cream is a timeless combination that lends itself to an assortment of treats. Since peaches can vary in sweetness depending on ripeness and season, we recommend taste-testing the smoothie before adding it to the Slush and Shake Maker. More agave nectar can be added to reach the desired level of sweetness. Peach schnapps is another way to enhance to the flavor, if desired.

Serves 2

INGREDIENTS:

2 cups (12 ounces) peeled and pitted peaches (3 to 4 large peaches)

3/4 cup half and half

1/2 teaspoon cinnamon

2 to 4 teaspoons light agave nectar

optional: 2 tablespoons peach schnapps, divided

DIRECTIONS:

Purée the peaches, half and half, and cinnamon in a blender. Add agave nectar to taste. Pour into the Slush and Shake Makers; stir until thick. Add 1 tablespoon schnapps, if using, to each Slush and Shake Maker. Stir to combine. The mixture will thin out; continue to stir until thick.

CHERRY
POMEGRA

There's nothing quite like a plump, fresh cherry bursting with tart juices. Pomegranate juice helps the tartness shine through the yogurt in this healthy, sweet and sour smoothie.

CHERRY POMEGRANATE **SMOOTHIE**

Serves 2

INGREDIENTS:

1 1/2 cups plain yogurt

1 cup pitted cherries

5 tablespoons 100% pomegranate juice

4 teaspoons mild honey, such as Acacia

DIRECTIONS:

Purée the yogurt, cherries, juice, and honey in a blender. Taste for sweetness and add more honey as needed. Pour into the Slush and Shake Maker; stir until thick.

BANANA
CARAMEL
SMOOTHIE

BANANA CARAMEL SMOOTHIE

Caramel is a treat that can be slightly challenging, but very rewarding to prepare at home. If you've never made caramel, here is an important tip to keep in mind: the lighter the caramel, the sweeter the drink. As the caramel becomes darker, there will be less sweetness and more bitterness—not necessarily a bad thing. It can take a little practice to find the right balance of flavor, but this smoothie is well worth the effort! To simplify the recipe, combine the half and half with store-bought caramel sauce. To really excite your taste buds, try adding a pinch of salt to the blender to create a salted caramel smoothie!

Serves 2

INGREDIENTS:

3/4 cup half and half, warmed
1/4 cup granulated sugar
2 large bananas, peeled
optional: pinch of salt

DIRECTIONS:

Caramel sauce: Heat the half and half in a small saucepan or in the microwave, then set aside. Place the sugar in a medium saucepan over high heat. The sugar will melt along the edges first. Use a heat resistant spatula to stir and dissolve the sugar evenly. When the caramel is slightly darker than honey, carefully add the warm half and half; the mixture will immediately bubble up. Once it settles, stir to combine and pour carefully into the blender. Purée the caramel sauce, bananas, and salt, if using, first on low speed, then on high speed. Pour the mixture into a medium bowl. Cool, then chill mixture in the refrigerator until cold, about 1 hour. Pour into the Slush and Shake Maker; stir until thick.

KEY LIME AVOCADO
SMOOTHIE

If you love key lime pie, you are going to fall head over heels for this silky smooth, sweet and tangy smoothie. We let our creativity reign and leveraged the natural creaminess of avocados as a base for the filling. If that sounds unusual, we challenge you to give it a try—there is no trace of avocado flavor in this smoothie! If fresh key limes are unavailable in your area, you can find bottled key lime juice in most grocery stores.

Serves 2 to 3

INGREDIENTS:
1 1/4 cups half and half or whole milk
2 Hass avocados, peeled and pitted
1/2 cup key lime juice
1/4 cup plus 2 teaspoons light agave nectar
1/4 teaspoon vanilla extract
optional: crumbled graham crackers for garnish

DIRECTIONS:
Purée the half and half, avocados, key lime juice, agave nectar, and vanilla extract in a blender. Pour into the Slush and Shake Maker and stir until thick. Garnish with graham crackers, if using.

BANANA NUTELLA
SMOOTHIE

Chocolate. Hazelnuts. Bananas. These three ingredients come together in perfect harmony to create a yummy smoothie that is so rich it might as well be a milkshake! To lighten it up a bit, use whole or low-fat milk. For the ultimate in decadence, try making this smoothie with half and half or even heavy cream.

Serves 2

INGREDIENTS:

2 medium ripe bananas (approximately 10 ounces)

1 cup half and half or whole milk

1/4 cup chocolate hazelnut spread, such as Nutella

DIRECTIONS:

Purée the bananas, half and half, and chocolate hazelnut spread in a blender. Pour the mixture into Slush and Shake Maker; stir until thick.

ZOKU®

SLUSH
AND
SHAKE
MAKER

ROASTED STRAWBERRY BALSAMIC
SMOOTHIE

Have you ever tried roasting fruit? Just like with vegetables, roasting fruit enhances the flavor in a marvelous way. Balsamic and strawberries is a classic, yet exciting combination that comes together nicely with rich, buttery brown sugar in this unique, tasty smoothie.

Serves 2

INGREDIENTS:

**13 ounces strawberries,
(approximately 1 3/4 cups),
hulled and sliced in half**

2 tablespoons brown sugar

2 tablespoons balsamic vinegar

3/4 cup heavy cream

DIRECTIONS:

Preheat the oven to 400 degrees F. Toss the sliced strawberries with the brown sugar and balsamic vinegar until evenly coated. Spread in a single layer on a baking sheet. Roast the strawberries for 10 to 15 minutes, depending on size. They will become soft and slightly darker as strawberry juice spreads onto the baking sheet. Purée the strawberries with their juices and the cream in a blender. Chill in the refrigerator until cold. Pour into the Slush and Shake Maker; stir until thick.

ZOKU®

SLUSH
AND
SHAKE

LASSI

MANGO **LASSI**

Mango lassi is a drink commonly served in Indian restaurants that is gaining worldwide popularity. Mangoes can vary in sweetness, so taste the drink before adding it to your Slush and Shake Maker. If it could use a bit more sweetness, add the agave nectar one teaspoon at a time until it's just right.

Serves 2

INGREDIENTS:

1 1/2 cups (9 ounces) chopped, peeled and pitted ripe mango (approximately 2 mangoes)

1 cup plain Greek yogurt, such as Fage

1/3 cup half and half

optional: light agave nectar, to taste

DIRECTIONS:

Purée the mango, yogurt, and half and half in a blender. Taste and add agave nectar, if needed; blend again. Pour into the Slush and Shake Maker; stir until thick.

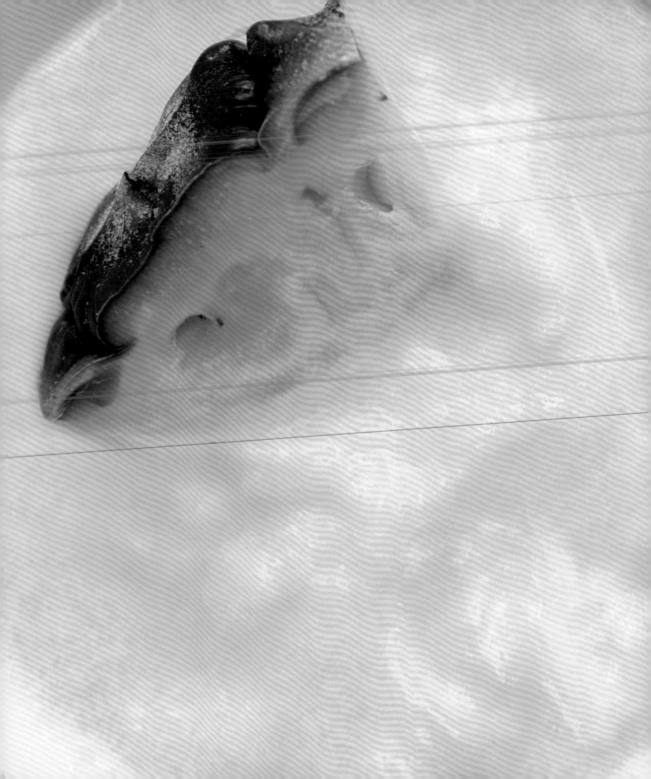

PIÑA COLADA
SMOOTHIE

If you like piña coladas...then I'm the smoothie that you've been looking for! Piña coladas evoke images of summer, vacation, sunshine, and tropical destinations... all good, relaxing thoughts. With the Slush and Shake Maker it has never been easier to make frozen piña coladas at home. So make this frozen smoothie, close your eyes, and relax.

Serves 2

INGREDIENTS:

1 1/2 cups (8 ounces) peeled, cored, and chopped fresh pineapple

3/4 cup coconut milk

1/3 cup pineapple juice

optional: 1/4 cup coconut rum, such as Malibu, divided

DIRECTIONS:

Purée the pineapple, coconut milk, and juice in a blender until smooth. Pour into the Slush and Shake Makers; stir until thick. Stir 2 tablespoons coconut rum, if using, into each Slush and Shake Maker. Stir to combine. The mixture will thin out; continue to stir until thick.

PIÑA COLADA SMOOTHIE

index

CONVERSION CHARTS

VOLUME

US	UK
1/4 tsp	1.25 ml
1/2 tsp	2.5 ml
1 tsp	5 ml
1 Tbsp / 3 tsp	15 ml
1 fl oz / 2 Tbsp	30 ml
1/4 cup	60 ml
1/3 cup	80 ml
1/2 cup	120 ml
1 cup	240 ml
1 pint / 2 cups	475 ml
1 quart / 4 cups	950 ml
1 gallon / 4 quarts	3.8 liters

LENGTH

INCHES	CENTIMETERS
1/4	0.6
1/2	1.3
1	2.5
2	5.1
3	7.6
4	10.2
5	12.7
6	15.2
7	17.8
8	20.3
9	22.9
10	25.4
11	27.9
12	30.5

OVEN TEMPERATURE

FAHRENHEIT	CELSIUS	UK GAS MARKS
200	95	-
250	120	1/2
275	135	1
300	150	2
325	165	3
350	175	4
375	190	5
400	200	6
450	230	8
500	260	10

WEIGHT

US	UK
1 oz	28 g
4 oz (1/4 lb)	113 g
8 oz (1/2 lb)	227 g
12 oz (3/4 lb)	340 g
16 oz (1 lb)	454 g